KAKADU NATIONAL PARK

FRONT COVER: Endemic Black Wallaroos can sometimes be seen from the Gunwardewarde Lookout at Nourlangie Rock.

OPPOSITE TOP: During the wet season waterfowl such as egrets, ibis and cormorants nest communally in large riverbank rookeries.

*OPPOSITE BELOW: The lily, **Crinum uniflorum**, flowers briefly during the early wet.*

ABOVE: Although rarely seen during the colder months, the Frilled Lizard is common in Kakadu.

Contents

The Flower of the Lotus Lily.

ACKNOWLEDGEMENTS

Thanks are due to a number of people including many of the excellent staff in Kakadu National Park. Marika Behr and Kate Duigan checked the text and Margaret MacGregor supplied the photograph on page 72. Special thanks are also due to Kakadu's traditional Aboriginal owners, many of whom checked the photo selection for me. In addition I wish to thank my patient wife Jane and my good friend Ian Morris. Jane provided technical and general support whilst Ian provided the photo on page 15 as well as photographic inspiration. David Lancashire and John Gollings supplied the photo on page 73.

Published and distributed by Barker Souvenirs, P.O. Box 2626, Alice Springs NT, 0871, Telephone (08) 89525277.

Design and Typesetting by Jane Moore, Environmental Media, P.O. Box 86 Jabiru, NT 0886.

Printed by Buscombe Printers, Melbourne, Victoria, Telephone (03) 9574 9000.

ISBN 0 646 28093 7

THE PARK

About 140 kilometres east of Darwin along the Arnhem Highway is the major entry to Kakadu National Park. Occupying an area of almost 20,000 square kilometres, Kakadu is jointly managed by the Australian Nature Conservation Agency and the Aboriginal owners of the region.

Kakadu has been declared a World Heritage Area, one of only 17 listed in the world for both natural and cultural values. Each year thousands of visitors come to experience the wildlife, the cultural legacy, the drama of the tropical seasons and the wild landscapes.

Four landscapes characterise Kakadu. The sandstone of the Arnhem plateau, the forested lowlands, the floodplains and finally the coast. Clothing these landforms are communities of plants which further divide the Park into numerous sub-landscapes including small patches of monsoon rainforest.

ABOVE: Not all of Kakadu's points of interest are ancient. The Bowali Visitor Centre is very modern and popular.

THE STONE COUNTRY

Thought to date back as far as 2,500 million years, some of Kakadu's base rocks are amongst the oldest on the planet. Overlaying these rocks is the sandstone Arnhem Land plateau. Known as the Kombolgie formation, this geological feature was laid down approximately 1,500 million years ago. The western edge of this plateau forms a near continuous line of cliffs, the escarpment, which stretches some 500 kilometres north to south. This spectacular plateau is comprised of deeply dissected gorges and ravines which edge wide rock platforms. Although attaining heights of only 500 metres, the plateau contains a wealth of spectacular scenery.

When the wet season deluge ceases, the turbulent waters disappear. This leaves behind a virtual sand and rock desert which bakes without relief for up to eight months each year.

OPPOSITE : In places primeval valleys, filled with dense monsoon forest, dissect the plateau.

ABOVE: The icon of Kakadu. Although spectacular during the wet, Jim Jim Falls can only be seen in this state from scenic flights.

Waterfalls in Kakadu shrivel to a trickle for much of the dry season. These watercourses originate on the impervious sandstone plateau. They rush and tumble to the lowlands through narrow U-shape gorges or via a series of cascades and breathtaking waterfalls such as Jim Jim and Twin Falls.

ABOVE: Stone country such as this is the exclusive home of the many species of plants and animals that are not found elsewhere.

OPPOSITE TOP: Beyond the escarpment and on the tabletop plateau are countless gigantic rock gardens of exquisite beauty. The poor quality sandstone soils collect precariously in shallow depressions and crevices in which more than twelve species of tough endemic plants grow. In the wet season these crevices and ravines are transformed into violent racing cascades. The waters slow only when they pour onto the flat lowlands and dump massive loads of sandy silt.

OPPOSITE BELOW: As seen here on the Bardedjilidji Walking Trail, the sandstone in the north of Kakadu weathers to beautiful shapes.

The western face of the Arnhem plateau extends north-south for hundreds of kilometres. This fascinating escarpment is on the path of wet season scenic flights.

TOP: Sometimes described as jungle, small patches of monsoon rainforest exist mainly in the gorges of the plateau and escarpment. They can also be found at the fringes of the floodplains where the high water table allows dense plant growth. These forests are relatively scarce and easily damaged by feral animals, weeds and wildfires.

BELOW LEFT: Thousands of minor waterfalls plunge from the plateau to the lowlands.

BELOW RIGHT: Where water seepage persists on the cliffs, a rich blanket of ferns and mosses emerges.

Sandstone Flora

The sandstone scrub and heath habitat is found on top of the dry sandstone plateau.

Here plants are tough, woody and sparse, and able to withstand the harshness of what is in effect a seasonal desert. Rainfall drains quickly from the sandy soils leaving stone country plants to cope in a severe annual drought.

As with animal species, it is in this landform that the highest number of endemic plants occur. Many species are found only in the stone country of Kakadu.

Imbued with gnarled character Basedow's Pandanus is one of three pandanus species found in the Park. This tree is restricted to the stone country where it is abundant.

*TOP: A large and spectacular sandstone tree is **Allosyncarpia ternata**. The canopy of this evergreen giant can form huge dense groves completely shading the forest floor. **Allosyncarpias** are damaged by repeated late season wildfires. Rangers endeavour to protect this species by burning surrounding country early in the dry season.*

BELOW: Prickly spinifex grass is the bane of bushwalkers. Many small animal species take shelter beneath its protective canopy.

TOP: Described by scientists in the mid 1980s this Mount Brockman Grevillea has gained popularity as an ornamental garden plant in Darwin.

BELOW LEFT: The Blue Berry Lily, is a small plant often found along sandstone creek banks.

BELOW RIGHT: Although found in many domestic gardens throughout north Australia the Carpentaria Palm is endemic to the Top End of the N.T.

TOP LEFT: ***Platysace arnhemica*** *prefers to cling precariously to the most precipitous cliff tops where it flowers prodigiously during the early wet season.*

TOP RIGHT: The native ginger appears only during the wet season and is seen at Ubirr and Nourlangie Rock.

BELOW: Along damp creek lines the native Lassiandra droops with dense flowerheads during the dry season.

Sandstone Fauna

Kakadu is home to impressive numbers of animal varieties as well as a marvellous array of endemic species, many of which have evolved in the sandstone country.

For millennia the plateau has been an ecological island surrounded by a sea of lowlands. This topographic isolation has led to the unique presence of animals such as the Black Wallaroo, Oenpelli Python, White-lined Honeyeater, Banded Pigeon, Chestnut-quilled Rock Pigeon and some species of frogs. Most sandstone animals spend the heat of the day tucked away in the vast subterranean network of caves or under rock ledges.

TOP ABOVE: The abrupt clatter of wingbeats is often the best guide to the presence of the endemic Chestnut-quilled Rock Pigeon.

ABOVE: Another Kakadu endemic is the White-lined Honeyeater whose piercing whistle echoes amongst the cliffs like a spirit of the stone country.

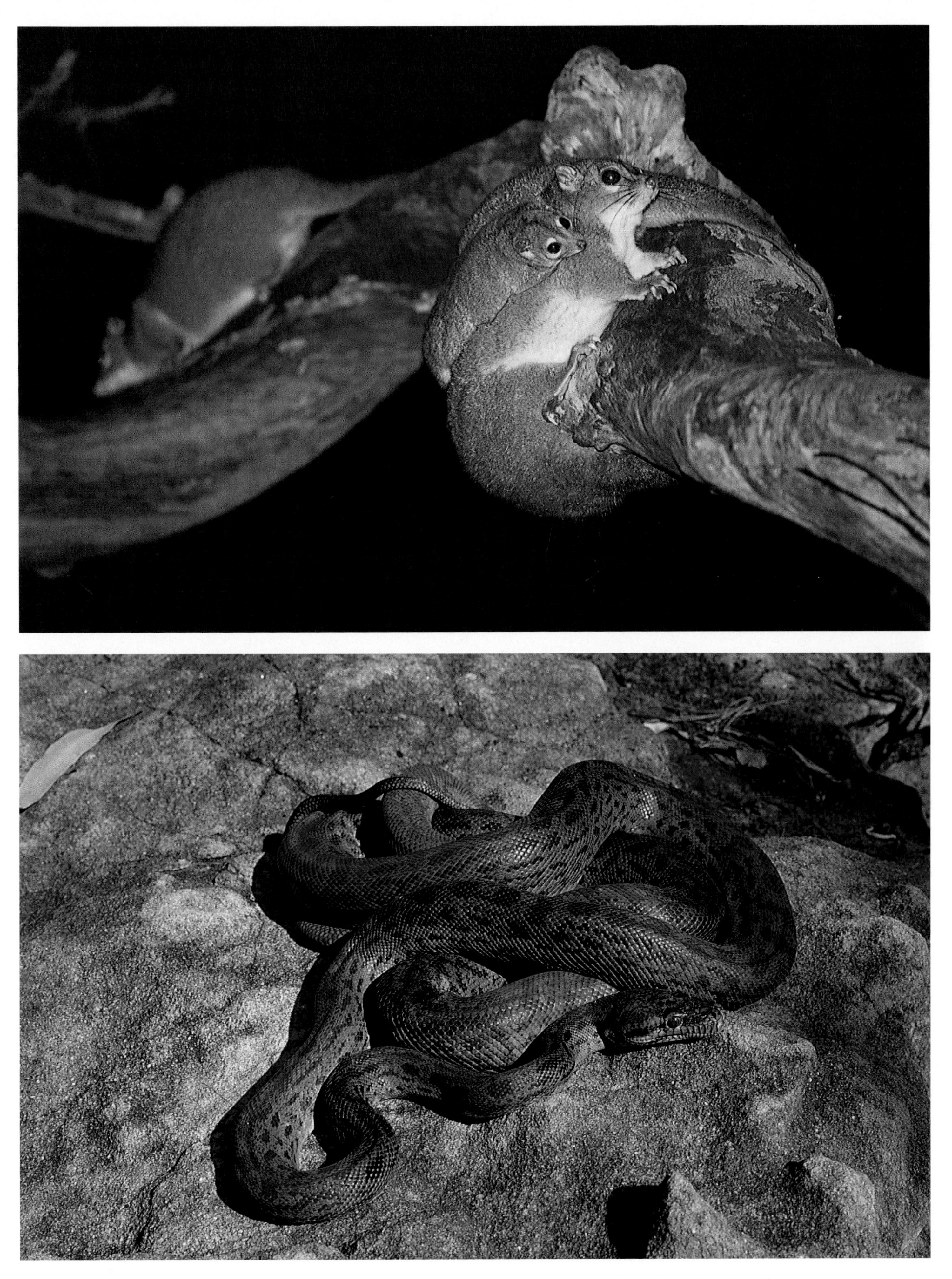

TOP: At night, particularly during the wet season, the sandstone country is alive with activity. Beautiful mammals such as the Rock Antechinus and the Rock Possum shown here, forage amongst the spinifex or the branches of trees. Frogs of many species call from the creek lines, while geckoes silently stalk insects among the bare rocks. *(Photo: Ian Morris)*

BELOW: The Oenpelli Python was unknown to scientists until 1977. The Aboriginal people know this 4 metre reptile as Nawaran.

TOP: Sandstone creeks and streams contain an impressive collection of fish species. The Saratoga is an ancient fish found in the tropical north of Australia.

BELOW: The Fire-tailed Skink is but one of a remarkable array of small reptiles inhabiting the Park.

TOP: The Kakadu Dunnart is a small carnivorous marsupial restricted to the south of Kakadu.

BELOW LEFT: A dweller of the dark monsoon forests, the Rufous Owl is a powerful nocturnal hunter which preys upon fruit bats and possums.

BELOW RIGHT: In Aboriginal mythology the gaudy Leichhardt Grasshopper is the child of Namarrgon *the Lightning Man.*

The animals of the sandstone country are closely tied to the ecology of the rocks. Most of them cannot survive even a few hundred metres away from this habitat.

THE LOWLAND FORESTS

Stretching to the north and west of the escarpment are the vast undulating lowlands which are thinly veiled in open forest. These lowland forests occupy the largest slice of the Kakadu landscape. Differences in slope, soil depth and type have created a subtle mosaic of vegetation types. In places tall open forests dominate, while elsewhere dense grasses are abundant, occasionally overlooked by short spindly paperbarks. Red apple trees and pandanus become common nearer the floodplain fringes.

Although less spectacular than the plateau country these forests are home to more animal and plant species than the other landscapes.

The drive into Kakadu gives rise to the impression that the Park is made up almost exclusively of lowland forest. The fact is that road builders avoid difficult country such as rocky areas, swamps and billabongs.

TOP: When viewed from the air the lowlands are seen as a vast carpet of interconnecting habitats.

BELOW: Early evening light casts a delicate hue over the lowlands in the mid dry season.

The abundance of plant and animal species in the woodlands is largely unnoticed, disguised by the apparent monotony of this vast habitat.

TOP: As the dry season tightens its grip in September, trees and shrubs drop most of their leaves allowing the fierce heat of the sun to bake the earth below.

BELOW: In contrast the wet season can bring temporary flooding of the lower reaches of the woodlands.

The presence of tall stands of Kentia Palms can be a surprise in otherwise continuous woodlands. Examples of this slow growing species can be seen at the roadside near Flying Fox Creek and the west branch of the West Alligator River on the Arnhem Highway.

Lowland Forest Fauna

High temperatures and intense tropical light drive most animals of the lowland forests into hiding. Only two types of snakes are regularly active during the heat of the day - the potentially dangerous western brown and the mildly venomous black whip snake. Sand goannas and several species of dragons, including the frilled, are the most commonly observed lizards. Balmy dry season nights suit a variety of lowland forest snakes such as Orange-naped snakes, the five species of pythons, and many species of lizards, particularly geckoes. This is also the time when mammals come into their own.

ABOVE: The Blue-winged Kookaburra is a raucous hunter of frogs, lizards, snakes and any other creature that it can overpower. The male can be identified by his blue tail, the female by her brown.

At night the fortunate observer may see Quolls, Fruit Bats and Sugar Gliders in the trees. Bandicoots, Brush-tailed Phascogales and native rats of several species skitter about on the ground. Occasionally an echidna will be seen shuffling along a roadside.

TOP LEFT: Black-footed Tree Rats forage on the forest floor retreating to tree hollows at dawn. These large fearless rats are well equipped with scimitar teeth and able to defend themselves against many predators.

TOP RIGHT: Propelled by a voracious appetite Northern Quolls scour the dark forest floor in search of smaller mammals, sleeping birds and other small creatures.

ABOVE: Pure breed Dingoes are common in Kakadu and can frequently be seen along roadsides. At dawn they patrol roads harvesting animals killed by traffic during the night.

TOP: During the dry season, when many trees are heavy with nectar filled flowers, Sulphur-crested Cockatoos become darkly smudged. This colour change can be attributed to them becoming coated with sticky nectar: when the birds land on the burnt earth the ash particles stick to their feathers.

BELOW LEFT: Orange-naped Snakes are one of several species of small colourful snakes found in the area. This species feeds on small lizards and frogs that are found beneath logs, rocky screes and old termite hills.

BELOW RIGHT: The personable Partridge Pigeon is most often seen and heard as a heart stopping blur when it erupts without warning into flight at one's feet. Although there are many in Kakadu this bird is becoming rare elsewhere in its range.

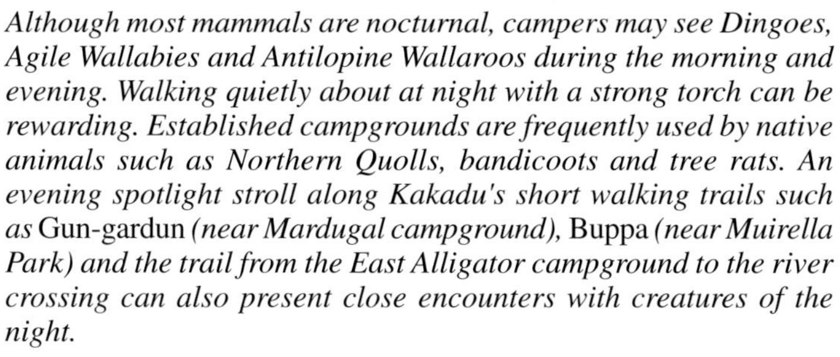

Although most mammals are nocturnal, campers may see Dingoes, Agile Wallabies and Antilopine Wallaroos during the morning and evening. Walking quietly about at night with a strong torch can be rewarding. Established campgrounds are frequently used by native animals such as Northern Quolls, bandicoots and tree rats. An evening spotlight stroll along Kakadu's short walking trails such as Gun-gardun *(near Mardugal campground),* Buppa *(near Muirella Park) and the trail from the East Alligator campground to the river crossing can also present close encounters with creatures of the night.*

TOP: Brush-tailed Phascogales are ferocious hunters among the woodland trees. They can be likened to carnivorous squirrels and are able to kill mammals as large as themselves.

BELOW LEFT: Whistling Kites have a piercing whistle which is a characteristic sound of the bush. They usually survive through scavenging but can be effective hunters if need be.

BELOW RIGHT: The beautiful Red-cheeked Dunnart is rarely seen but lives by hunting small animals under cover of the dense grass beside creeks and floodplains.

Lowland Forest Flora

Lowland forests constitute the largest single habitat in Kakadu. It is through this forest that the Arnhem and Kakadu highways pass. Despite its apparent monotony this is a rich habitat for plants and animals alike. The dominant tree species are the eucalypts and acacias. Most trees have their trunks and limbs hollowed out by termites. Although of little apparent benefit to the tree, this tunnelling is of extraordinary importance to mammals, birds, reptiles and amphibians. The hollowed trees provide nesting places and refuges for large numbers of woodland vertebrates and insects.

Scattered randomly amongst the trees of the lowlands is the Top End's sole representative of the pine family. The Cypress Pine is a species which suffers badly from late season fire. Skeletons of these trees stand as silent testimony to a bygone period of hot wildfires. Rangers devote considerable effort to preventing late season fires to minimise the risk to this and other embattled species. A healthy patch of Cypress can be seen along the Nourlangie Rock road.

TOP LEFT: Native speargrass is the fuel which feeds the annual fires in the Top End. A hot dry season fire does not affect the seeds of this grass because they bury themselves in the protective soil. From here they rapidly germinate after early wet season rain.

TOP RIGHT: The Fern-leafed Grevillea flowers during the dry providing copious quantities of nectar to woodland honeyeaters.

BELOW: Rangers are constantly required to identify the prodigiously flowering Kapok Bush which flowers throughout the dry season.

Most lowland plants flower during the dry season. With the passing of the rains many trees and shrubs respond by decking themselves in colours of every hue. This is time of plenty for nectar feeding insects, birds and possums.

TOP: The Turkey Bush only flourishes in areas of very poor soils where it flowers during the dry.

BELOW LEFT: During the wet season the small Purple Clover plant can form flower heads of striking beauty.

BELOW RIGHT: Most plants drop the bulk of their leaves in the dry season as a means of conserving moisture. The Kurrajong Bush flowers at this time.

Pandanus spiralis *is found throughout the woodlands of the Top End. Aboriginal people developed many uses for this plant.*

FIRE

Almost half of the lowland forests are burnt each year, the flames being fed by vast quantities of native speargrass. The relatively slow fires lit in the early dry season cause more good than harm while fires which occur later than August can damage the flora and fauna. The use of fire by Aboriginal people has been an integral part of this country for thousands of years and can be said to be the main architect of the contemporary landscape. Plants and animals alike employ a range of strategies to protect themselves from fire and its aftermath.

TOP: As soon as the grasses begin to dry, rangers take to the air dropping thousands of incendiary capsules on the woodlands. In this way technology mimics Aboriginal tradition.

BELOW: Kakadu rangers Grant Matson and Wayne Forde work a fire line in June. Early 'cool' fires such as this are rarely life threatening.

TOP: Aborigines light dry season fires to 'clean up the country'. These fires push back snakes and mosquitoes and make it easier to walk about in search of food.

BELOW LEFT: The central cone of the dry banksia flower will smoulder for hours. By using many of these cones people were able to carry fire over considerable time and distance.

BELOW RIGHT: Slow growing but persistent, Sand Palms can survive all but the most ferocious late dry season fires.

THE WETLANDS

In the north of Kakadu, away from the escarpment and towards the sea, the lowlands become increasingly interrupted by wide floodplains. These flank the major rivers and creeks and extend to the coast. Wet season flooding transforms these plains into inland seas which can exceed 15 kilometres in breadth. The fresh nutrients that are deposited enrich the soils each year. However floods make it difficult for forest giants to emerge and only a handful of species of trees have succeeded in capitalising on the riches of the floodplains. Only paperbarks have flourished on the combination of rich soils, annual drought and floods.

To the north, the floodplains are transformed into saline mudflats and meet the Timor Sea through a fringe of mangroves.

OPPOSITE TOP: Yellow Water is but one of many floodplain watercourses in the Park. This area has boat cruises which make it possible for visitors to appreciate the wetlands, and its wildlife at close quarters.

OPPOSITE BELOW: Annual flooding in February or March transforms the wetlands to inland seas.

ABOVE: The South Alligator River is Kakadu's pulsing artery. The entire river from source to sea lies within the National Park.

TOP: Covering more than 3,000 sq km of Kakadu, wetlands are made up of a complex pattern of river channels, billabongs and backwater swamps such as this one in the north of the Park.

BELOW: In contrast to the image conjured up by the name 'swamp', Kakadu's wetlands are full of colour and light.
Here the billabong is dominated by the tranquil beauty of the Lotus Lilies.

TOP: Late wet season floods coincide with a riot of flowers amongst paperbarks and lily pads.

BELOW: In contrast the dry season finds many paperbarks high and dry for months. Few species of trees can survive such extremes.

During September and October shrinking water levels on the flood plain yield vast beds of spike rush bulbs to the probing bills of Pied Geese. Tens of thousands of geese gather to feast at this odd time of plenty.

TOP: The absence of vegetation beneath the large paperbarks, combined with moist earth, generally protects these beautiful trees from the ravages of the late dry season fires.

BELOW: In places around the edges of the floodplains where fire does not penetrate, small pockets of monsoon forest persist. This example is Manngarre near the East Alligator River.

Wetlands Flora

During the wet season the floodplains explode in a riot of growth. Countless varieties of lilies, grasses, sedges and aquatic plants flourish. From this watery jungle emerge vast numbers of fish, frogs and insects which then become the diet of waterfowl and other wetland hunters. Later, during the long dry, the sedges and grasses, which grow from seeds or bulbs, die back and may even be burnt.

The soils of these plains are highly fertile because nutrients have been leached from the surrounding higher country and deposited onto the floodplains.

As floodwaters subside huge beds of sub-aquatic vegetation are revealed.

TOP: Lotus Lilies grace many a freshwater billabong. Eaten to near extinction by buffalo these lilies are now so abundant that they frustrate the efforts of anglers in some watercourses.

BELOW: Stately Leichhardt Trees sometimes form dense shade canopies reminiscent of groves of English oaks.

In geological terms the flood plains of Kakadu are very young. Cahill's Plain or Nardab *in front of the Ubirr lookout, is only 800 years old.*

The flood plains and their margins have always provided a welcome array of foods for the indigenous population. Bulbs, fruit, seeds, the roots and stems of lilies, yams, spike rush and other water plants can provide a year round feast. Yegge *and* Gurrung *(mid to late dry) are particular times of plenty.*

TOP LEFT: The Silver-leafed Paperbark flowers between May and August.

TOP RIGHT: The Freshwater Mangrove flowers at night and in the early hours of the morning sprinkles a bright red carpet of fallen flowers on the ground below.

BELOW: The large Kapok Tree grows along tidal riverbanks and in patches of monsoon forest. The flowers attract many species of nectar eating birds.

TOP: As the floodwaters retreat large areas of Yellow Snowflake Lilies flower. Scenes such as this have contributed to Kakadu wetlands being included on a list of the world's significant wetlands.

BELOW: Spring fed jungles contain a rich collection of unusual plants such as the palm, ***Hydrostele wendlandiana,*** *and a variety of tree and ground orchids.*

Weeds

Kakadu is not without its misfits. A number of alien weeds threaten this country, the most sinister and destructive of which tend to colonise the wetlands. But, despite this, only 5% of Kakadu's plant species are alien, making this park one of the most weed free in the world.

The worst of these threats is a small thorny tree called the Giant Sensitive Plant, *Mimosa pigra,* which has been kept out of Kakadu by a vigilant team of specialist rangers whose task it is to seek and destroy this vegetative curse. The floating water fern, *Salvinia,* has invaded some stretches of Kakadu waters.

TOP: Next to Cane Toads, the greatest environmental threat to Kakadu's wetlands is the Giant Sensitive Plant.

*BELOW: Kakadu is the only place in Australia where the **Mimosa** scourge is under control. This is largely due to the efforts of a few dedicated people such as Joye Maddison, seen here destroying a seedling plant.*

*TOP: The floating fern, **Salvinia molesta**, originally from South America, is a threat to the lagoons and billabongs. It blankets the water surface, denying oxygen and light to the plants and creatures below. Here, two members of the Park's weeds control team, Buck Salau and Michael Storrs, inspect **Salvinia** on Magela Creek.*

*BELOW LEFT: In Kakadu the weed **Salvinia** has been subjected to a steady assault with biological control in the form of both a weevil and also strategic spraying with herbicide. A balance has been achieved with **Salvinia** only gaining the upper hand during prolonged dry seasons and poor wet seasons.*

BELOW RIGHT: There are no practical methods of control for pasture grasses, such as Para and Gamba Grasses, which invade flood plains and exclude native plants. Rangers try to quarantine Kakadu from the arrival of such weeds by inspecting and pressure water cleaning any earth-moving machinery arriving in the Park.

Wetlands

Fauna

During the dry season huge flocks of waterfowl assemble on the edges of the floodplain billabongs. The wetlands are also the main habitat for many species of frogs. During the early wet the mating calls of these personable creatures can be deafening.

Annual flooding allows fish to breed in astounding numbers and disperse throughout the wetlands in a boom and bust cycle. Fifty two species of fish ranging from the tiny freshwater 'blue eyes' to 8 kg Salmon-tailed Catfish, have been identified in the Park. Barramundi can weigh in at 20 kgs and are much pursued as a sport and table fish.

At places such as Yellow Water, Magela Creek and the Wildman River, Pied Geese, spoonbills, Brolgas and Glossy Ibis congregate. This spectacle occurs during the dry season when receding waters expose huge quantities of food in the form of sedges, bulbs, fish and frogs. The birds move from one drying billabong to another in a pattern that has been repeated annually for thousands of years.

OPPOSITE: After the vast flat floodplains have dried rock hard in November, Pied Geese can no longer easily feed and therefore live on accumulated fat. Here they bide time at a shallow billabong awaiting the rains which will provide them with new grass so they can graze on the plains.

ABOVE: Tough times for geese can be a time of plenty for the Jabiru. Near dry billabongs in the late dry expose large numbers of fish to the Jabiru's deadly bill.

TOP: Brolgas nest on the ground during the wet. Here a pair is seen courting in mid dance.

BELOW: During the dry season Wandering Whistle Ducks gather in huge numbers in remote areas of the wetlands.

TOP: Only the female Pig-nosed Turtle ever comes ashore, and then only briefly, to lay perfectly round hardshelled eggs in the white sand banks of sandstone creeks and rivers.

BELOW LEFT: Glossy Ibis gather where small fish congregate in watercourses.

BELOW RIGHT: Black Fruit Bats often form camps, which include thousands of individuals in shady monsoon forests. From here they fly for considerable distances each night in search of flowering and fruiting trees.

TOP: The Saltwater (or Estuarine) Crocodile is common in all watercourses from the sea to the larger pools in the sandstone gorge country. When young these ancient creatures eat frogs, crustaceans and small fish. At 2 to 3 metres they feed almost exclusively on fish. Once they exceed 3 metres in length they begin to take mammals such as wallabies and dingoes. Very large crocodiles frequently feed on mammals. Large 'salties' can reliably be seen from the boat cruises at Yellow Water and on the East Alligator River throughout the dry season.

BELOW: Freshwater Crocodiles are generally found in the upper reaches of rivers where they can occur in high numbers. This species often mixes with 'salties' but must keep a very low profile to survive.

The arrival of Europeans during the last century saw a change in the fauna of the country when new species spread in the region. Native wildlife found it very difficult to compete with exotic animals. Asian Water Buffalo found Top End floodplains very much to their liking. During the past decade the Australian Government has orchestrated the removal of these mild mannered creatures in an attempt to eradicate the diseases brucellosis and tuberculosis from Australia.

TOP & BELOW: Although buffalo numbers in Kakadu have been reduced from some 60,000 to less than 200, feral pigs remain abundant. Feral horses, cats and European honey bees also continue to be a problem in Kakadu. Moves are afoot to deal with pigs and horses while the cat is the subject of a concerted research effort. Perhaps the greatest environmental threat to Kakadu comes in a small package. It is estimated that the Cane Toad will arrive in Kakadu by the year 2000.

THE COAST

A dry season visit to West Alligator Head reveals beige sandy beaches dotted with dense shade trees, their leaves disturbed by gentle breezes. A tall, dark backdrop is created by pockets of monsoon forest which have emerged around the freshwater soaks tucked behind the dunes. It is not unusual for crocodiles to clamber laboriously over the foredune to lie in these waterbodies before returning to the sea.

During high tide the turquoise sea laps invitingly at the shoreline. Swimming is out of the question as large crocodiles patrol offshore, occasionally snapping up a stingray. These rays occur in large numbers and, concealed by the turbidity and the curling waves, enjoy nothing more than foraging at the waters edge. On shore, sandflies can be very irritating with no relief from their biting until sundown when they are replaced by mosquitoes.

OPPOSITE: The coastal region can be complex. On the landward side of the shallow opaque sea lies a thin band of sandy beach. Behind this monsoon forest and tall paperbacks ring freshwater soaks. Further inland the thick monsoon forests abruptly give way to eucalypt woodlands.

ABOVE: Although coastal beaches are accessible at West Alligator Head, most of the seaward fringe of Kakadu is lined with an impenetrable wall of mangroves.

ABOVE: Mangroves and jungle almost meet, separated only by a slim line of beach sand.

OPPOSITE TOP: Black Wattles stabilise the dunes but their wide tangle of roots are a curse for turtles attempting to dig safe repositories in the sand for their eggs.

OPPOSITE BELOW: Huge tides of up to eight metres can inundate the beach area and threaten to poison the freshwater soaks behind the foredunes.

The tropical seas are home to strange animals such as Flatback Turtles, Saltwater Crocodiles, Dugongs, Barramundi, and countless crabs. Brahminy Kites and White-bellied Sea Eagles soar over the waters. Clustered in the shade of the tree tops, Black Fruit Bats restlessly eye the eagle which poses a deadly threat. Mangrove Kingfishers and herons stalk amongst the lower branches of the mangrove forest as they hunt for fish. On the mud below White-bellied Mangrove Snakes and Little File Snakes forage for crabs and fish. At night during low tides Water Rats rush about feeding on molluscs and crustaceans before the returning tide blankets this food source.

TOP: Although Flatback Turtles doggedly return to Kakadu's beaches to nest each year most eggs are lost to large goannas which are skilled at finding and raiding the fresh nests.

BELOW: Commercial fishing in Kakadu is now outlawed, giving Mud Crabs a degree of protection not found elsewhere.

TOP: The large and powerful White-bellied Sea Eagle is a versatile hunter. Its preferred diet includes fish, file snakes, turtles and fruit bats. This mature bird is seen here with an Agile Wallaby.

BELOW: At the other extreme, the diet of the petite White-bellied Mangrove Snake is very restricted. It feeds almost entirely on small crabs.

Coastal Flora

The coastal fringe is dominated by mangroves which are continuously trapping suspended mud and colonising it into new mudbanks. Inexorably they march northwards into the Arafura Sea at the rate of 20 to 30 cm per year. Mangroves are widely recognised as being the cradle of our fisheries. Important species of commercial fish and crustaceans breed in the sanctuaries that are formed by vast areas of tidally inundated and tangled mangrove roots. Kakadu has 112 kilometres of coastline most of which is comprised of mangrove forests. This coast is protected from clearing and other forms of development.

TOP: Where a laterite ridge meets the mouth of the South Alligator River the branches of mangroves and woodland eucalypts almost touch.

BELOW: Spider mangroves stand in the mud on elaborate aerial roots.

TOP: Some of Kakadu's largest patches of monsoon forest are found adjacent to the sea.

BELOW: Mangroves such as ***Avicennia*** *and* ***Ceriops*** *can be found well upstream on the banks of tidal rivers. Kakadu has a surprising number of species of mangrove, 21 varieties being found in the Park. These are not the spindly dwarfs found on the southern coasts. Top End mangroves are often robust and tall and always richly coloured. One deciduous species even turns on delightful autumnal hues before dropping its leaves.*

THE KAKADU CLIMATE

The weather in the Top End swings between extremes. The annual drought of eight months is shattered in November by violent electrical storms which herald the arrival of the monsoon with its flooding rains. 1.7 metres of rain can fall in little more than three months.

The Aborigines of the region identify six distinct seasons. During *Gudjewg* the monsoonal deluges of the mid wet season span January to March. The last storms flatten the vast areas of speargrass during April, the 'knockem down' season called *Bang-gereng.* The relatively cool dry period of May and June is called *Yegge,* while *Wurrgeng* is the "cold" weather months of June and July. August to September becomes unbearably hot and is known as *Gurrung.* During the 'build up' season, *Gunumeleng,* increased humidity leads to the savage storms of October till December.

For some Park residents the height of the wet is the most spectacular of all seasons. Limited access puts scenes such as Ubirr in flood beyond reach of visitors.

TOP: The effects of the Gudjewg *floods are most impressive on the wide floodplains.*

BELOW: As the monsoon eases in March violent electrical storms return in time to 'knock down' the tall annual speargrass.

TOP: As the waters recede in April, lilies of many species come into flower in beautiful wide swathes of colour.

BELOW: By May columns of smoke herald a long period of broadscale burning.

TOP: In September the country is once again in the grip of the annual drought.

BELOW: By November the cycle is complete with wild electrical storms announcing the return of the wet.

KAKADU ROCK ART

Along with the flora and fauna of Kakadu the stone country is internationally acclaimed for its wealth of rock art. The galleries at Ubirr, Nourlangie Rock and Nanguluwur showcase excellent examples of the many art styles to be seen in the region.

Galleries are most numerous in areas where the sandstone meets the floodplains, a measure of the abundance of food and shelter in these areas. Caves and overhangs with a high density of paintings were usually occupation sites, places where the entire community lived.

Heavily painted sites are not necessarily sacred or ceremonial places. Sacred or dangerous sites are usually associated with a specific physical or topographical feature.

TOP: Estimated to be about 30,000 years of age, simple monochrome (one colour) prints of hands and other objects are thought to be Kakadu's oldest art form.

BELOW: As much as 10,000 to 15,000 years old, pre-estuarine paintings reflect the drier climate of that time and often depict kangaroos, echidnas and emus. Beautiful small paintings of humans in action were also executed during this period.

TOP: Although dating back to 4,000 years, the decorative x-ray paintings are considered a relatively recent style. Bush tucker was often depicted and subjects included fish, turtles and the wallaby shown above.

BELOW: As recent as 300 years old, 'contact paintings' record the first encounter with non-Aboriginal people and depict rifles, horses, buffalo, boats and even aeroplanes. There are examples of art in the East Alligator area which were painted in 1985.

Ubirr

Ubirr overflows with cultural and natural wealth. Elaborate images decorating the walls of occupation shelters reflect the history and animal life of the area. Few places in the world offer such an easy lifestyle to traditional people.

With food, water and shelter all around, Aborigines have had time to develop a rich and complex culture, elements of which are skilfully painted on the many rock faces of the Ubirr site.

OPPOSITE: A build up storm broods over Ubirr.

TOP LEFT: Ubirr has excellent examples of 'contact' paintings: here a white man stares authoritatively down from the main gallery.

TOP RIGHT: This decorative x-ray painting depicts a turtle.

BELOW: This remarkable Thylacine (Tasmanian Tiger) painting accurately illustrates an animal which has been presumed extinct on mainland Australia for 3,000 to 5,000 years.

Nourlangie Rock

Along with Ubirr and Nanguluwur, Nourlangie Rock offers some of the finest indigenous art to be seen anywhere in the world. Elevated boardwalks make exploration of the various galleries and shelters easy and informative. The depths of the Anbangbang Cave amply demonstrate the comfort of a cool occupation shelter as opposed to the heat of the surrounding country.

TOP: The view of Nourlangie Rock from the nearby Nawurlandja lookout at sunset is stunning.

BELOW: Nabulwinjbulwinj is an important Spirit Being in the Nourlangie area. Along with the main frieze of paintings, this image was retouched by a traditional artist in the mid 1960's. Retouching of art is unusual.

TOP LEFT: A recent surprise discovery by archaeologists has shown that bees wax images such as this can be as many as 4,000 years old - thousands of years older than expected.

BELOW: The main gallery illustrates spiritual beings as well as people. Namarrgon, the Lightning Man, can be seen on the right.

TOP RIGHT: Over time many paintings have lost their stories. This jumble of images may have been painted piecemeal over a very long period.

Nanguluwur Gallery

At the end of a 1.7 kilometre walk is one of Australia's finest art sites. Nanguluwur is best visited in the morning while the main rock face is in cool shade.

High on the spectacular cliffs above the boardwalk are impossibly placed paintings. The old people tell us that these were painted by Mimis. Mimis are slender fragile spirits which live in narrow rock crevices and emerge during calm weather.

TOP: This painting of a fully rigged sailing ship is a fine example of contact art and is less than 1,000 years old.

BELOW: Some intriguing and dramatic paintings of female spirit figures grace the rock walls of Nanguluwur.

THE PEOPLE

Archaeological evidence suggests that people have been living in the Kakadu area for as long as 60,000 years. Some of the old people recall camping as children in sites that contain evidence of uninterrupted occupancy for as many as 24,000 years. Prior to European arrival there may have been up to 3,000 people living in the Kakadu area.

Today 300 Aboriginal people live in the park area, their lifestyles ranging from suburban through to tiny outstations in remote areas near the escarpment.

The lands of Kakadu supported a highly mobile population. Aboriginal culture was and continues to be, complex. This culture requires adults to fulfil serious responsibilities in relation to religious ceremonies and rites as well as traditional laws, along with social and economic obligations.

The first regular contact Aborigines had with people from other lands appears to have occurred when Macassan sailors arrived on the northern shores. Their praus *(sailing boats) were propelled here by the northwest monsoon. The Aboriginal people readily adopted some of the Macassan ways, pipe smoking being amongst them. Many Macassan words were included in the Aboriginal language.*

In the early 1800's the Dutch were replaced by the English as the most frequent mariners around northern Australia. Whereas the first 'contact' paintings were of the Macassan praus, the more recent depict items of English origin. Rifles, figures dressed in western style clothing, axes and horses were amongst these.

ABOVE: Bluey Ilkirr is widely recognised as one of Kakadu's best artists.

OPPOSITE: Bluey's wife Susan Aladjingu is skilled at craft work and makes a range of items from hand made string.

Since the time of early western contact major events have overtaken the people of the Alligator Rivers region. The most important recent event was the discovery in the late 1960's of rich uranium deposits at Jabiru, Jabiluka, Nabarlek and Koongarra.

The subsequent mining at Jabiru and Nabarlek has opened a technological and cultural floodgate. With compulsive speed this has propelled the region's original inhabitants from a quiet backwater right into the mainstream of Australian society. Today traditional land owners are consulted on a broad range of issues in the region and are the key decision makers in Kakadu.

ABOVE: Aboriginal people are closely involved in the management of Kakadu. Senior Ranger Victor Cooper is seen here working with fire in the early dry season.

(Photo Margaret MacGregor)

TOP & BELOW: The Warradjan Aboriginal Cultural Centre near Cooinda was opened in 1995. The Centre showcases Aboriginal traditional and contemporary history as well as illustrates their profound knowledge of the land. An hour spent in this building is very valuable. (Bottom Photo by John Gollings, courtesy David Lancashire Design).

KAKADU TODAY

Kakadu has changed dramatically in recent years. The completion of the Arnhem Highway in 1974 allowed direct access from Darwin because major bridges now crossed the creeks and rivers.

Prior to this, the area was a tough two day drive from Darwin. The few small settlements in the region used to be marooned for months each wet season and supplies were flown to those fortunate enough to have an airstrip.

Things are very different today. Kakadu is now in the Australian mainstream combining a modern town, lavish hotels and lodges set in a wild landscape.

A glimpse of cliffs of the Arnhem Land plateau can be seen from the town's supermarket doors. These cliffs are part of the Arnhem plateau which is largely unexplored.

TOP: In the town of Jabiru visitors can stay in a remarkable hotel built in the shape of a saltwater crocodile. Cheaper and less luxurious accommodation is available at the Frontier Lodge.

BELOW: The Ranger uranium mine is an important element of the region's economy. This mine is highly regulated in order to ensure that environmental problems do not occur. Aborigines who are owners of the affected area have formed associations which receive royalties from this mine. The money has been used to invest in the tourism industry through purchases such as the Crocodile Hotel, the Cooinda Lodge and the Yellow Water boat cruises.

TOP: Opened in 1994, the Bowali Visitor Centre won Australia's most prestigious architectural award. The 170 metre building contains a cafe, souvenir shop, library, an audio visual area and an elaborate display. For seven days per week during business hours, staff are available to provide the latest information about such things as what to do and road conditions.

BELOW: The Frontier Holiday Village near the South Alligator River is one of two excellent condominium style hotels in Kakadu. The other is the Cooinda Lodge near Yellow Water.

THINGS TO DO

Not surprisingly, a park as large as Kakadu has plenty of activities to offer visitors. Things to do vary according to the season with the cooler dry months providing the greatest range of options. Between May and November the dry season offers more than fifty destinations.

Apart from occasional periods of peak flooding, access to the Yellow Water boat cruises, the Nourlangie Rock and Nanguluwur art sites, Gunlom Falls and various lookouts and walking trails is generally possible throughout the wet season.

Time is the biggest enemy of the Kakadu visitor. It is difficult for people to comprehend the size of this Park before they arrive. Three day's touring is quickly consumed by seeing the main attractions. It is only after this that visitors can get 'off the beaten track' and explore Kakadu's back country.

TOP: Yellow Water is world renowned for its wildlife especially crocodiles. This cruise showcases the rich wetland habitats.

BELOW: At the East Alligator River a very different cruise is offered. This is a cultural cruise with Aboriginal guides explaining and demonstrating various handicrafts. The environment features tall sandstone cliffs, white sand beaches and both species of crocodile.

TOP: The Jabiru olympic pool offers safe swimming in north Kakadu. To the south, swimming is popular at Gunlom and Maguk Gorge which is shown here.

BELOW: Also popular in the south of Kakadu are extended overnight bushwalks. Permits are required in advance from the Park Visitors' Centre.

TOP: Viewing sunsets from various lookouts is a serene, contemplative way to end the day.

BELOW: Kakadu has hundreds of kilometres of remote area bush tracks. Naturally these are only trafficable during the dry season.

TOP: Kakadu is a wildlife photographer's paradise with special opportunities available at Yellow Water.

BELOW: Fishing has been popular and rewarding in Kakadu for thousands of years. Be aware that certain restrictions apply in the Park. A Park Note on fishing is available from the visitor centre.

KAKADU NATIONAL PARK

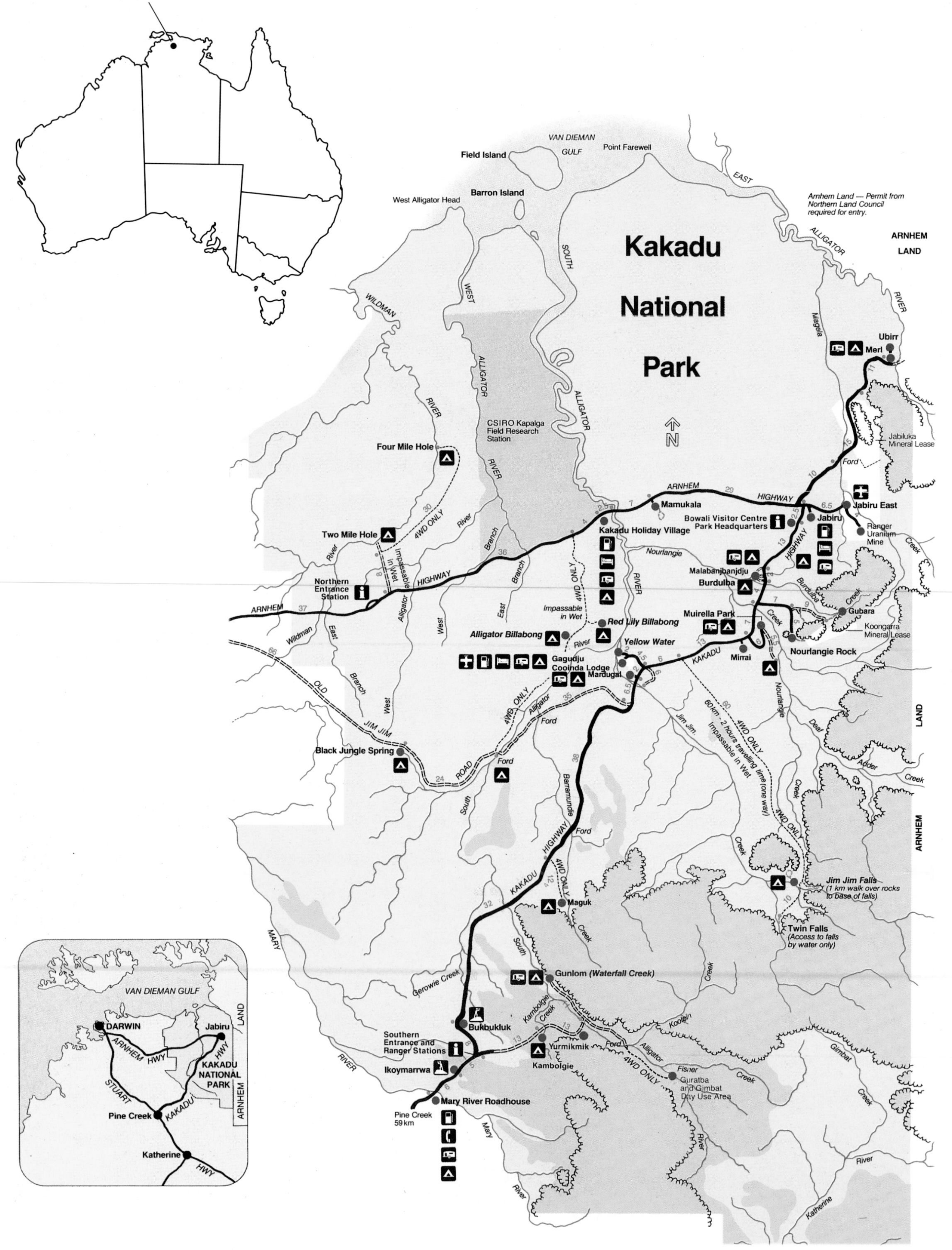